I0756881

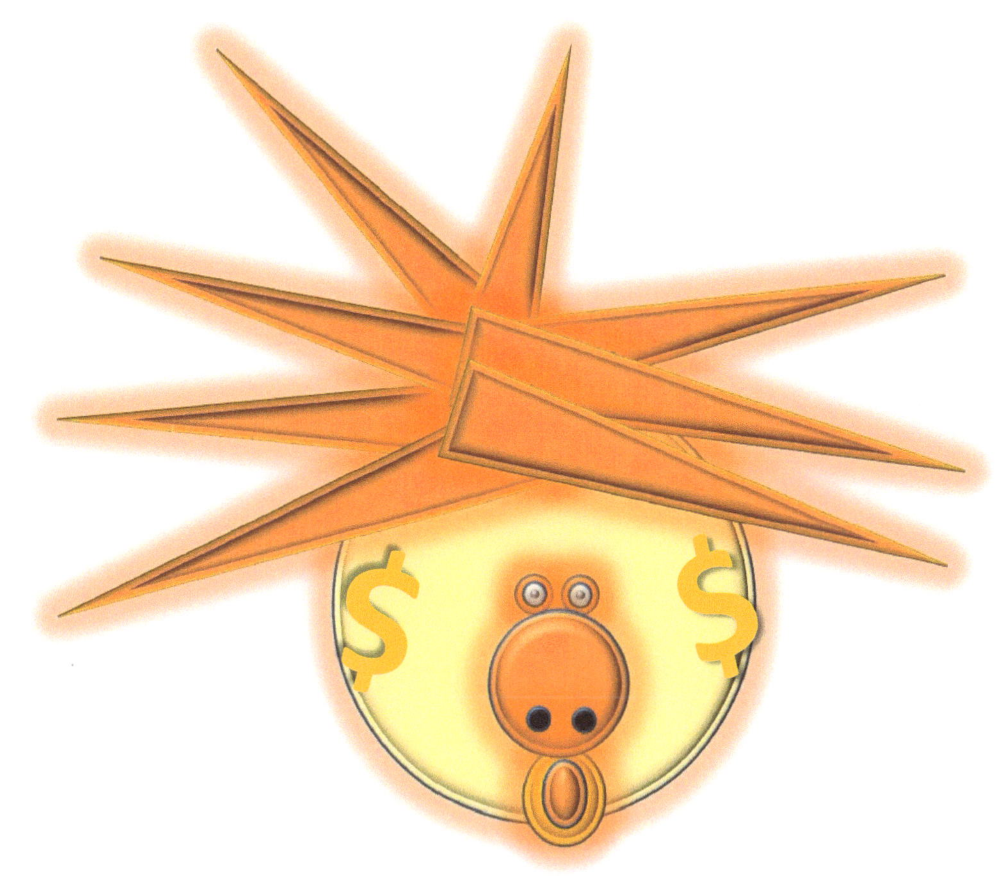

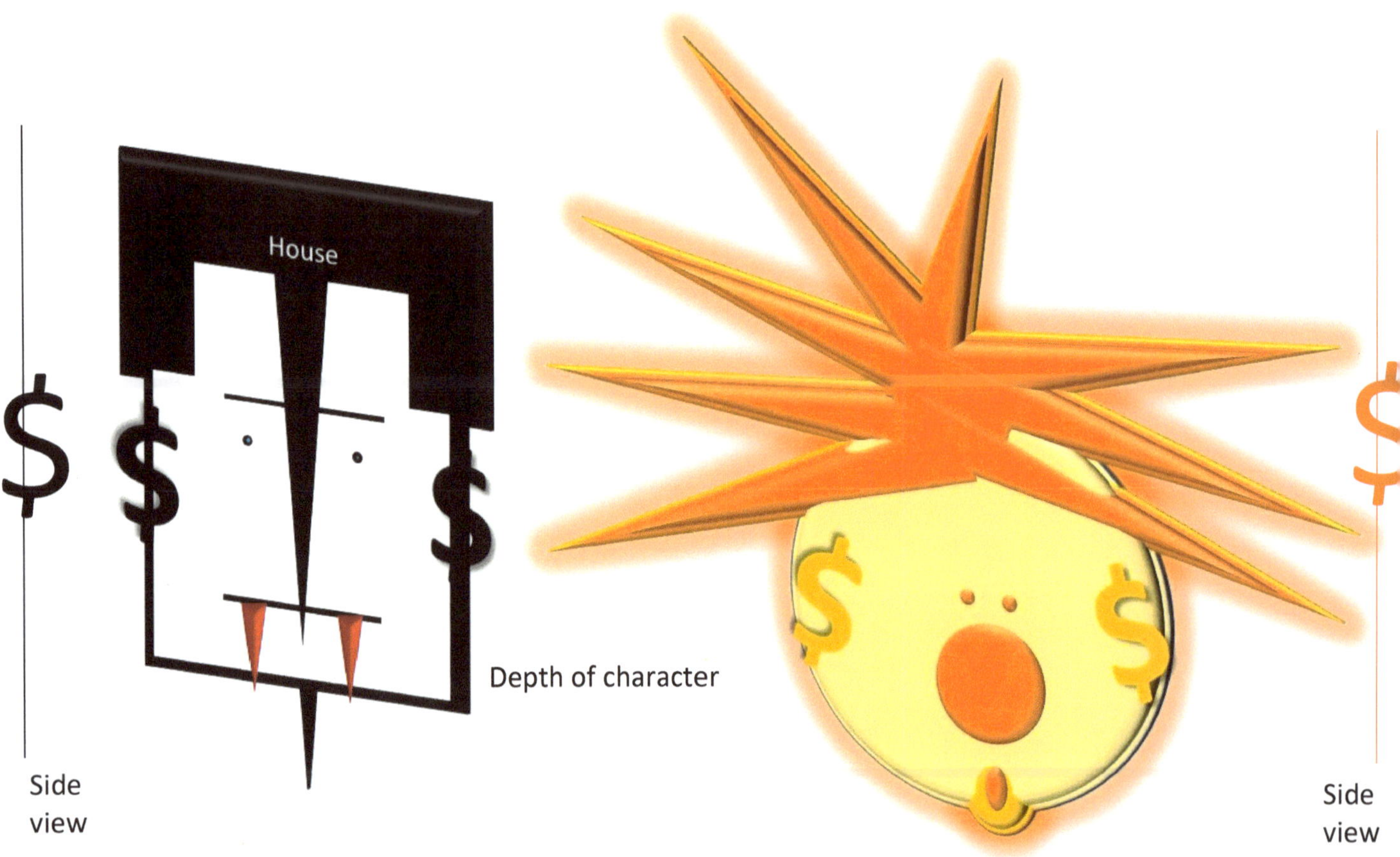
House
Depth of character
Side
view
Side
view

The **Wrecking**
Ball Diaries

Starring

DJT

PR

T

K E dV

Apologies to Miley Cyrus

(resemblance pure coincidence)

By

Zachary F Burton

Dr. Z, PhD

House

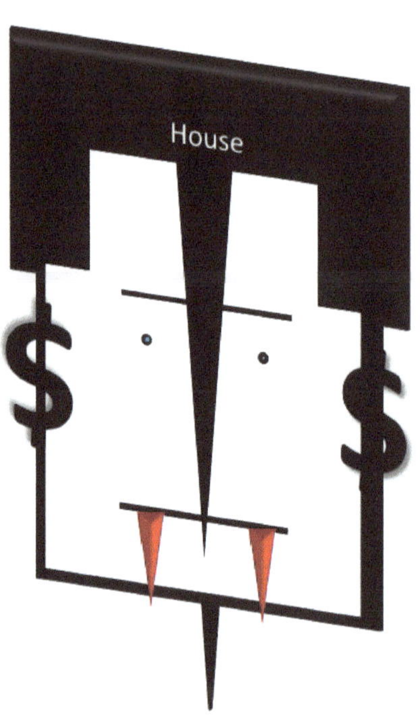
House

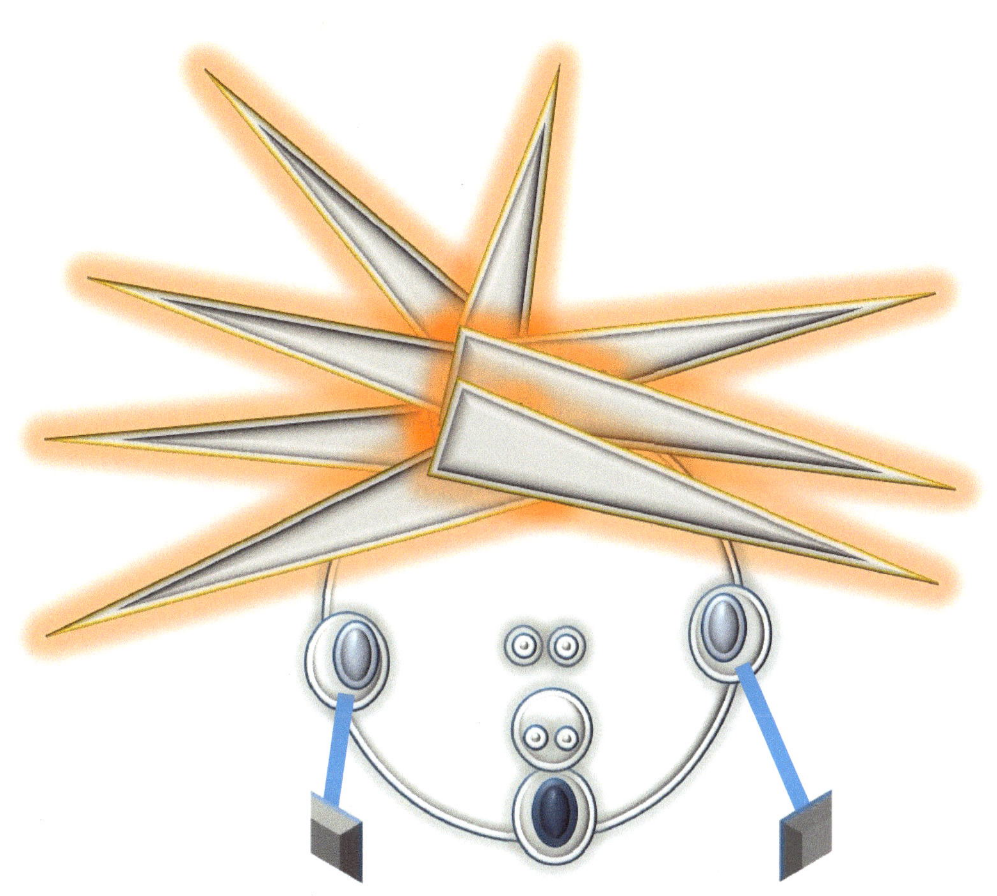

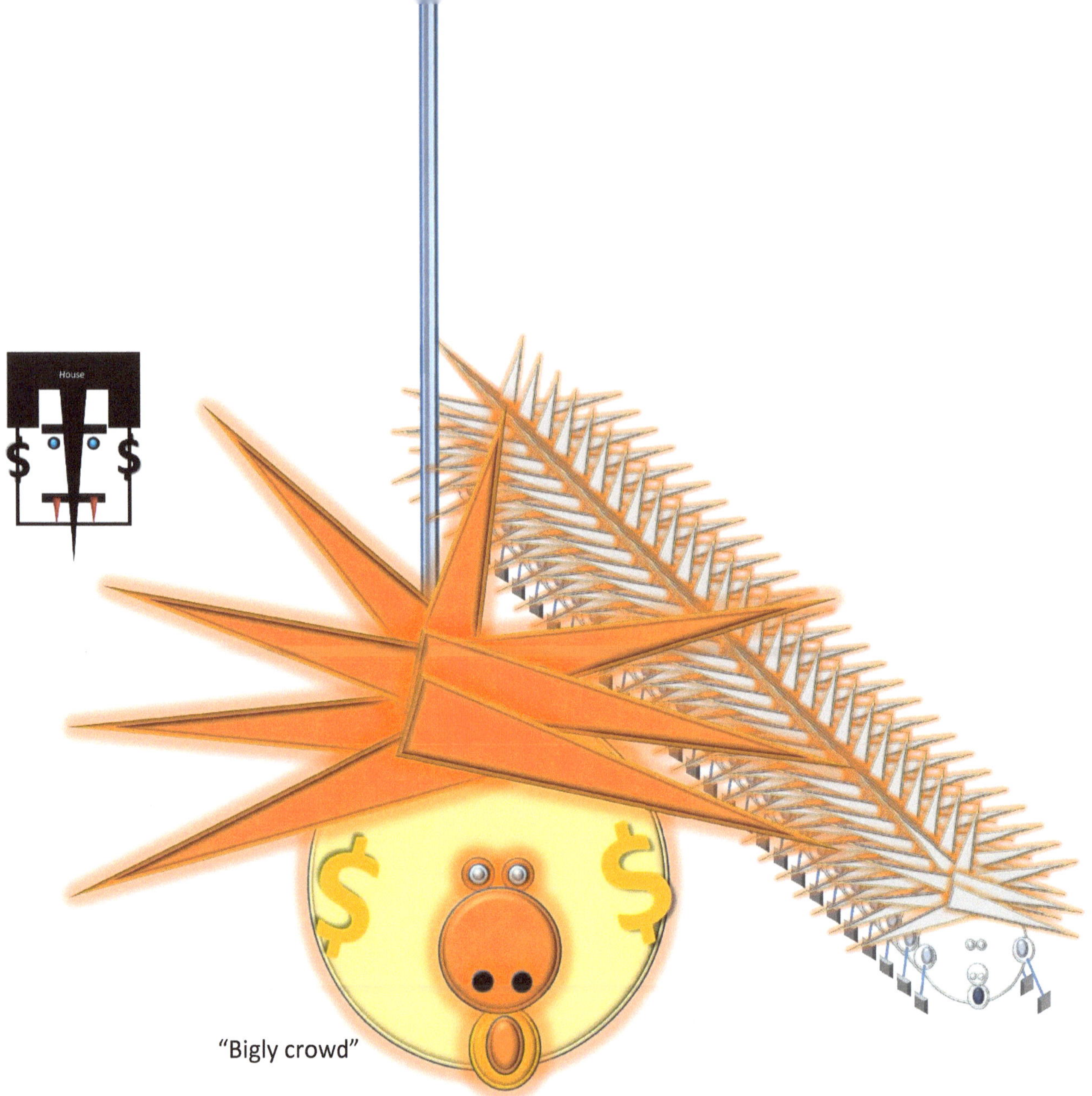
House
"Bigly crowd"

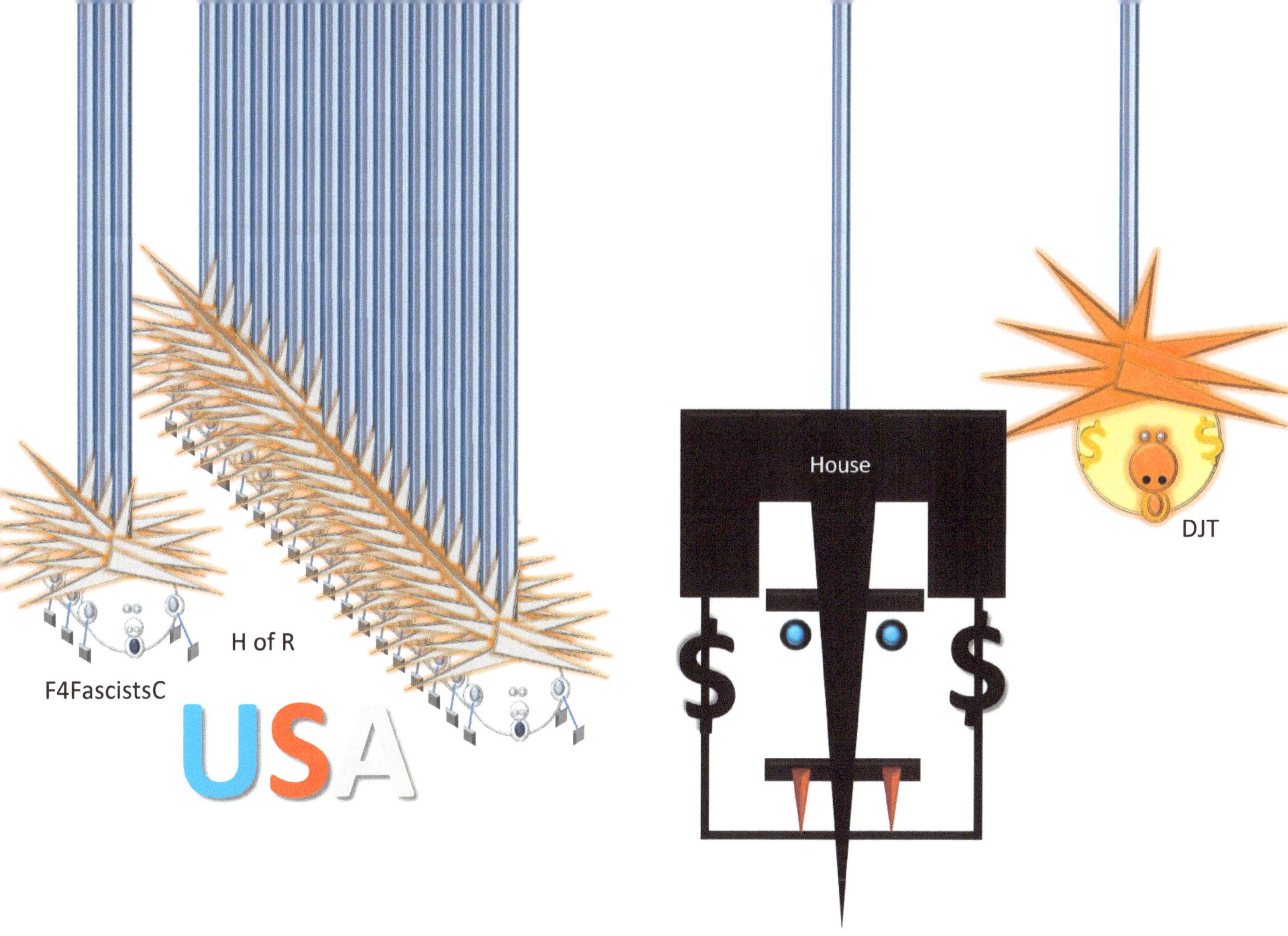

F4FascistsC
H of R
USA
House
DJT

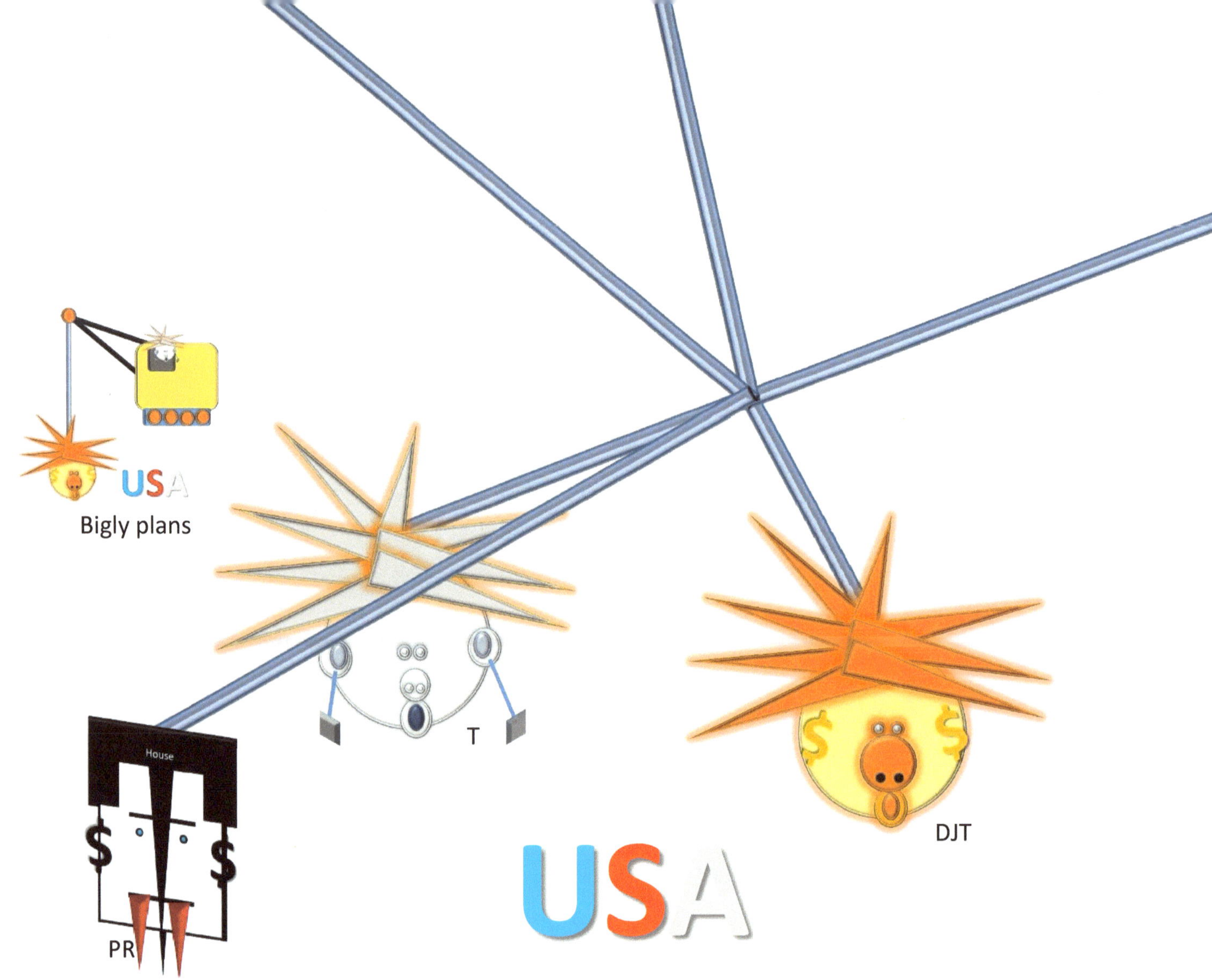

USA
Bigly plans
House
$
$
PR
T
USA
DJT
"We got tangled"

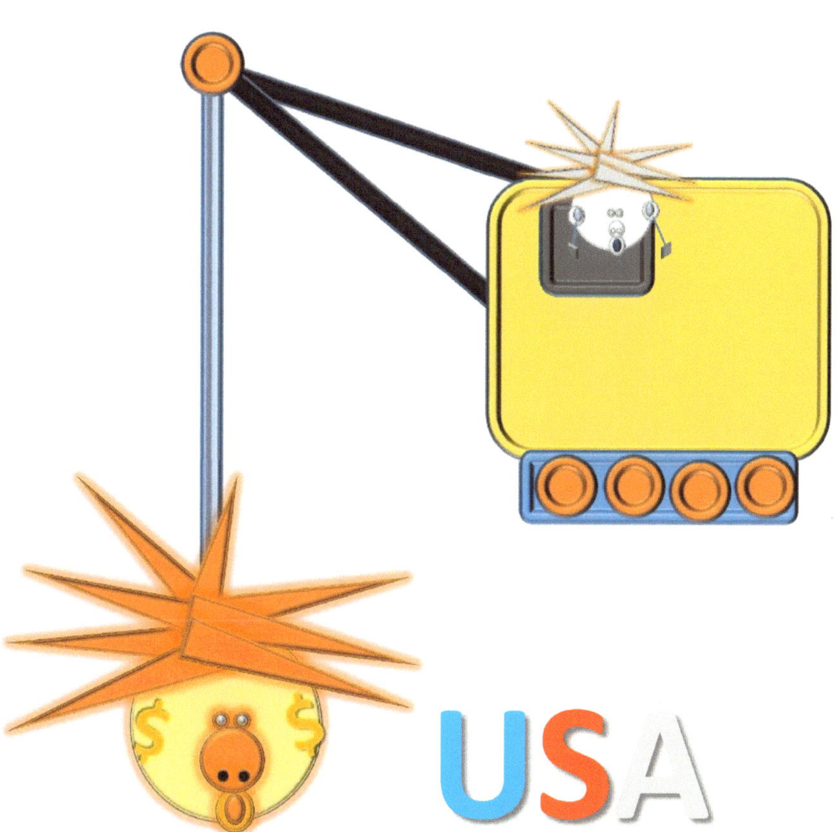
USA

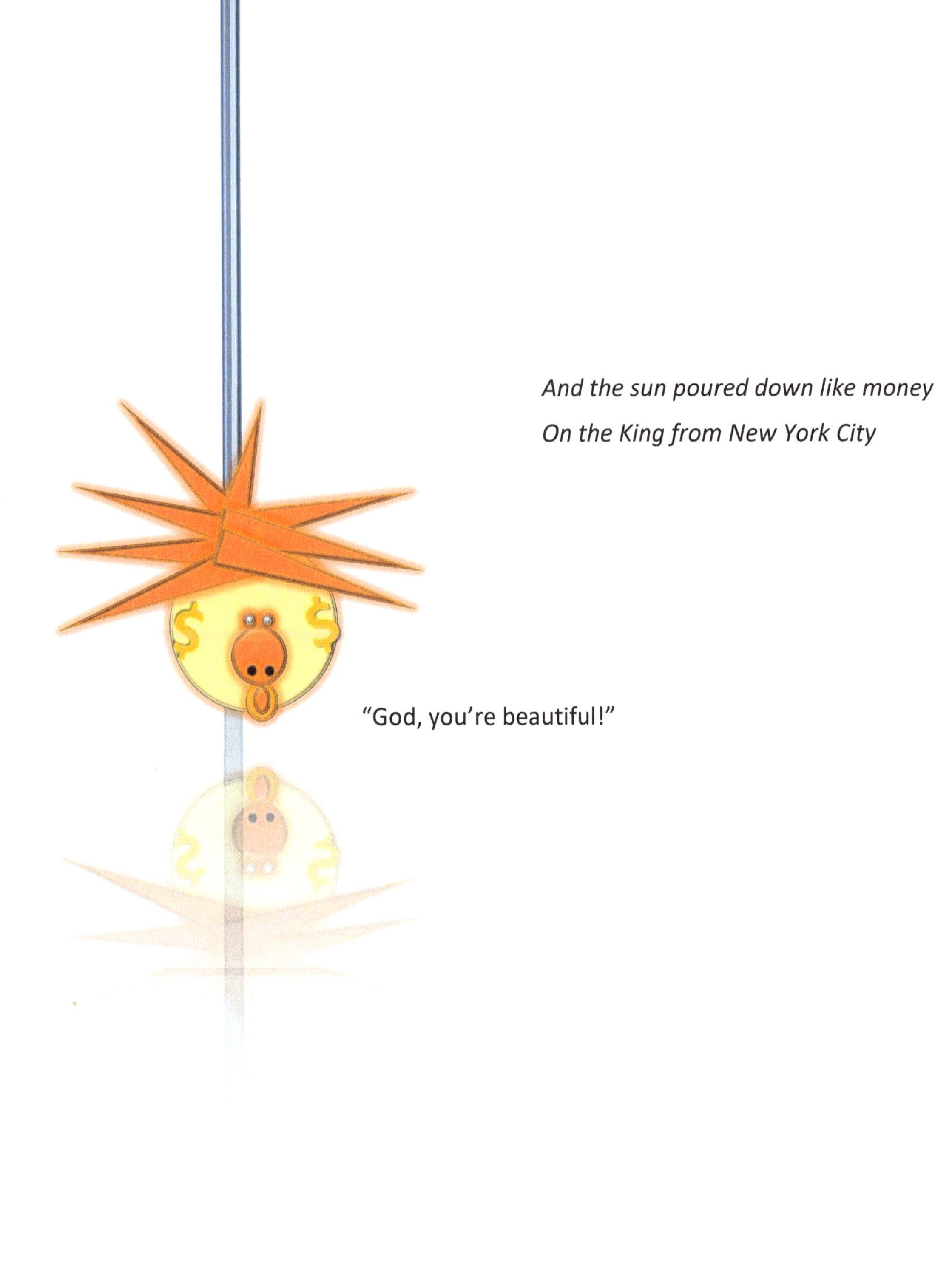

And the sun poured down like money

On the King from New York City

"God, you're beautiful!"

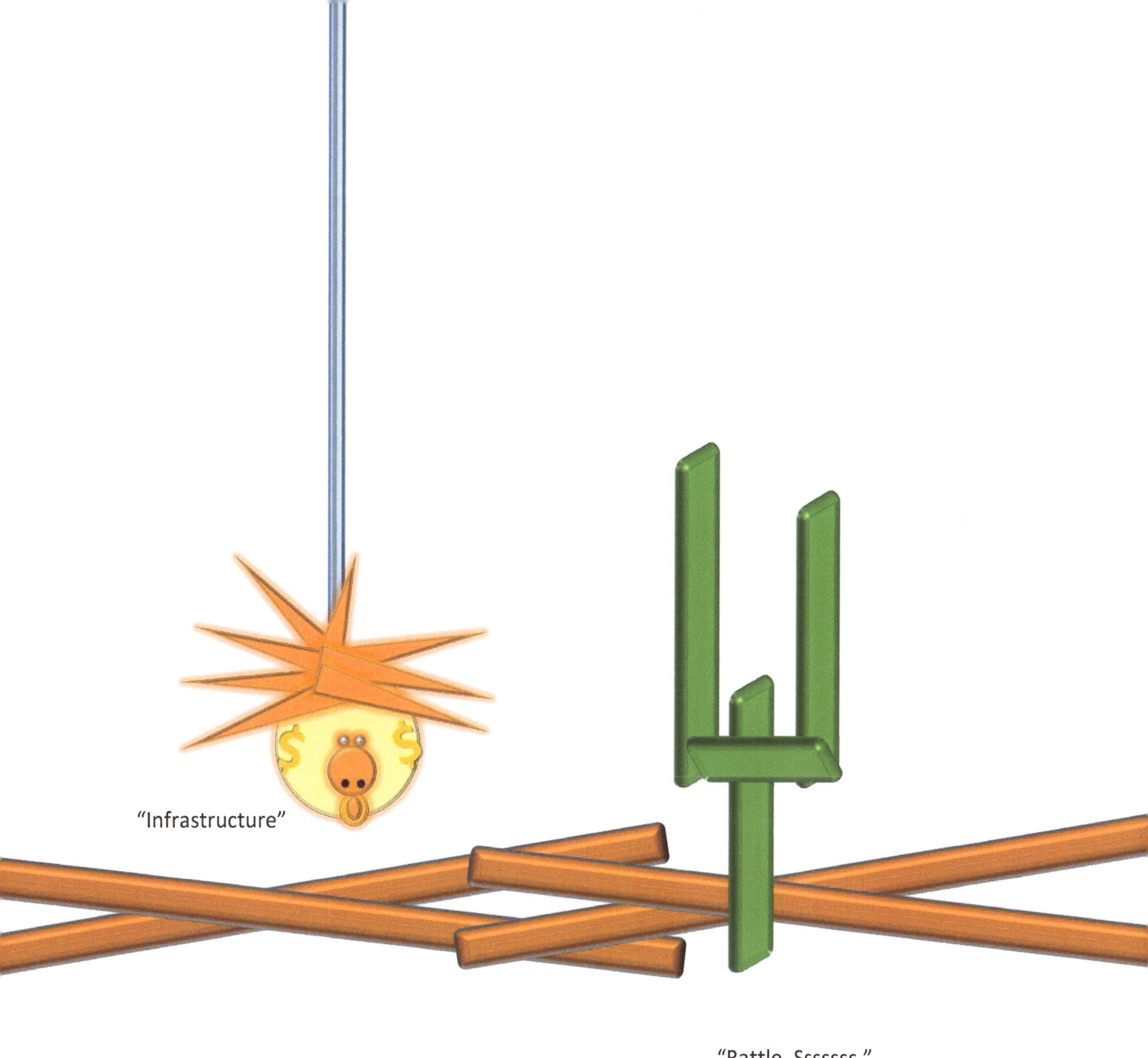

"Infrastructure"
"Rattle. Sssssss."

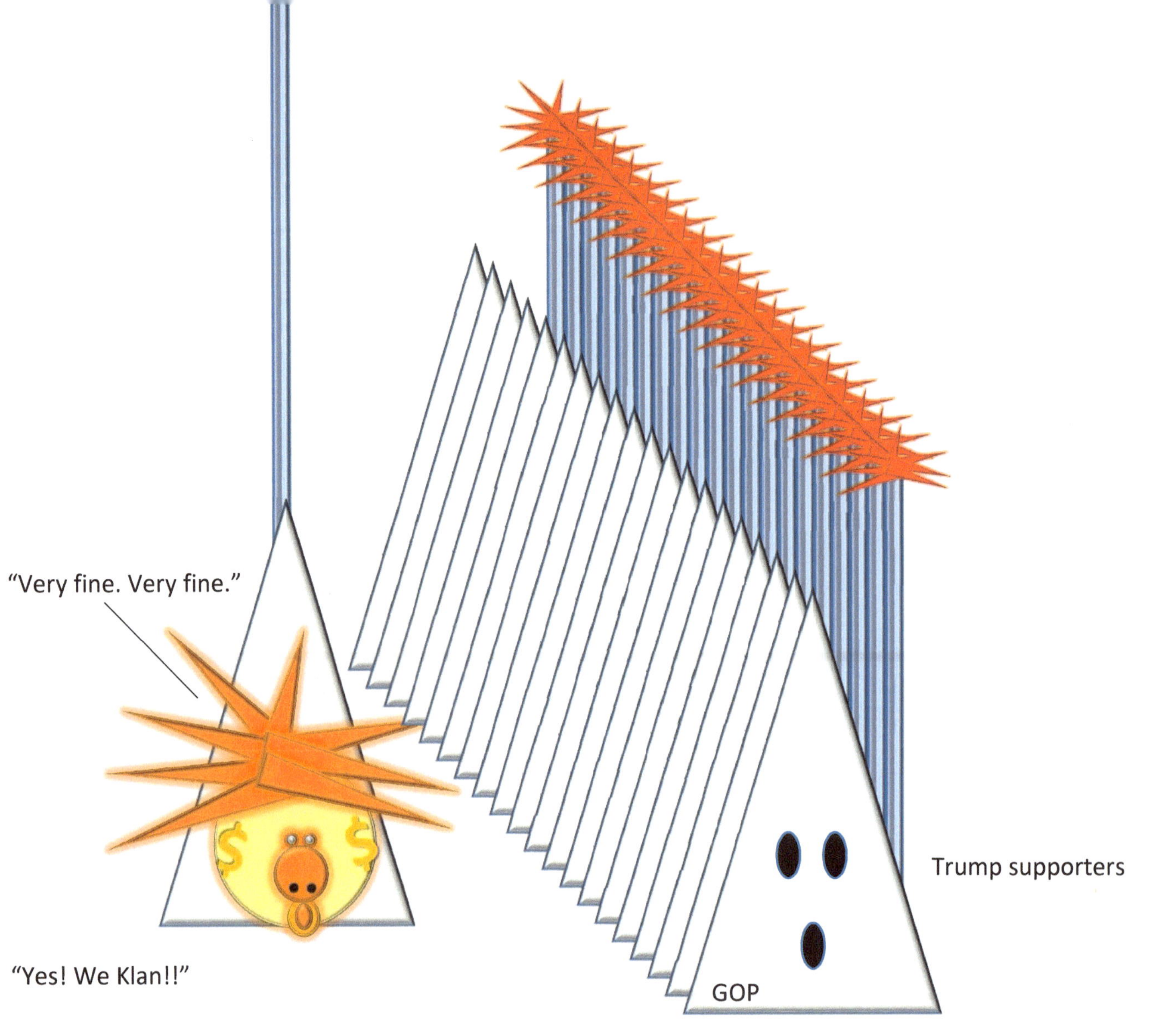

"Very fine. Very fine."
"Yes! We Klan!!"
Trump supporters
GOP
Motto of: GOP, DJT, PR, MMc, KKK, Nazis, Tea, traitors, fascists, etc.

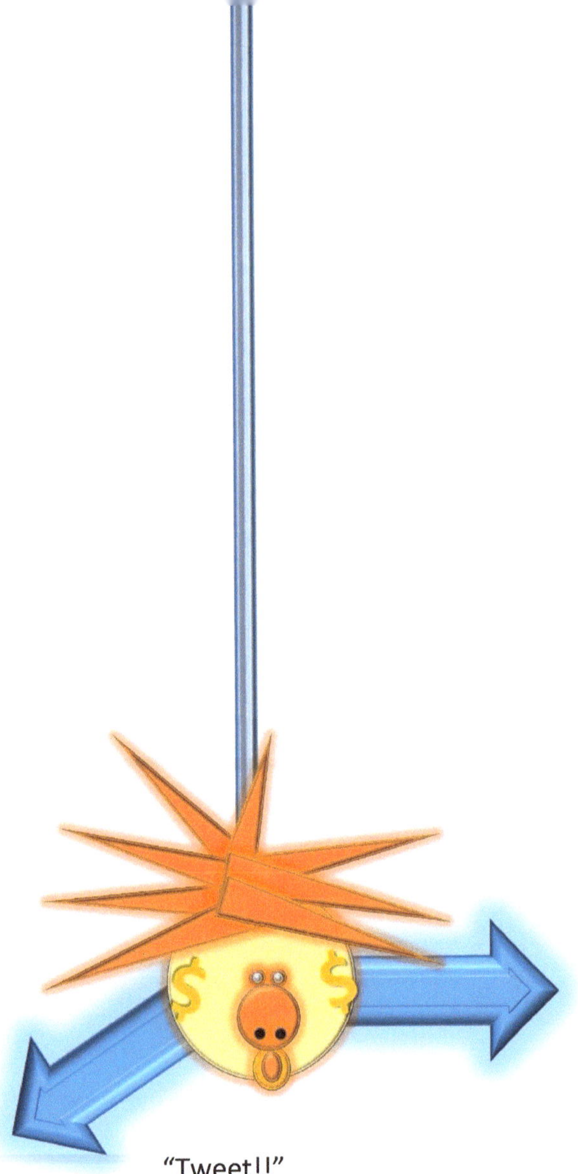

"Tweets have wings."

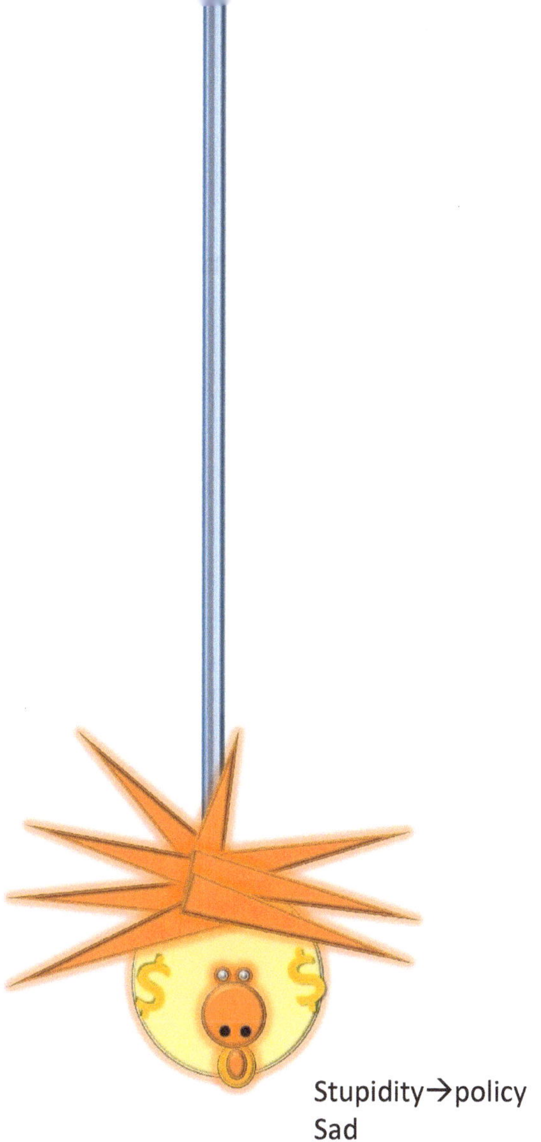

Stupidity→policy
Sad

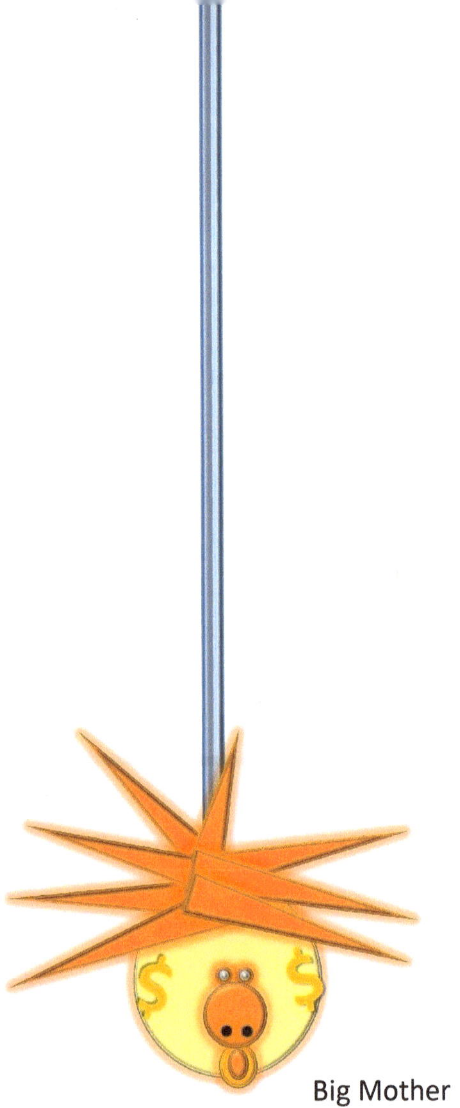

Is watching

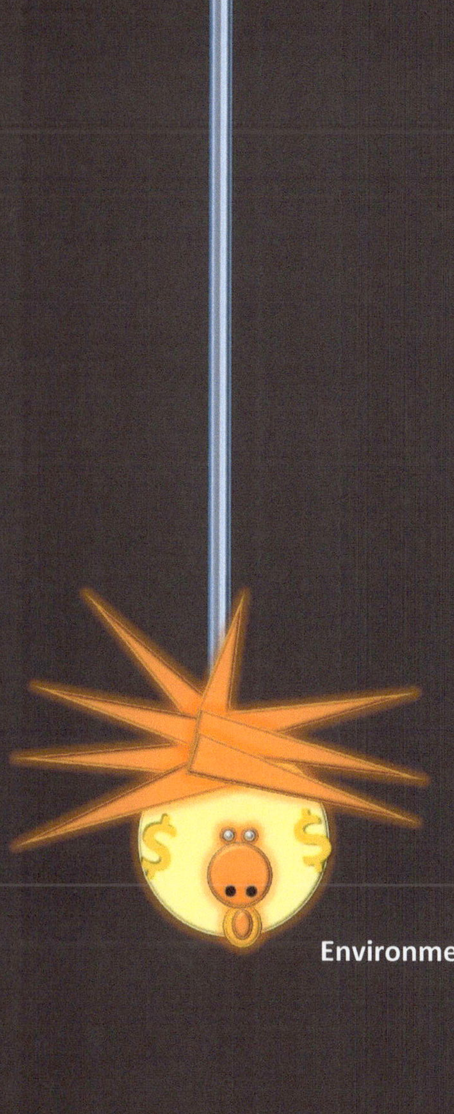

Environmental policy

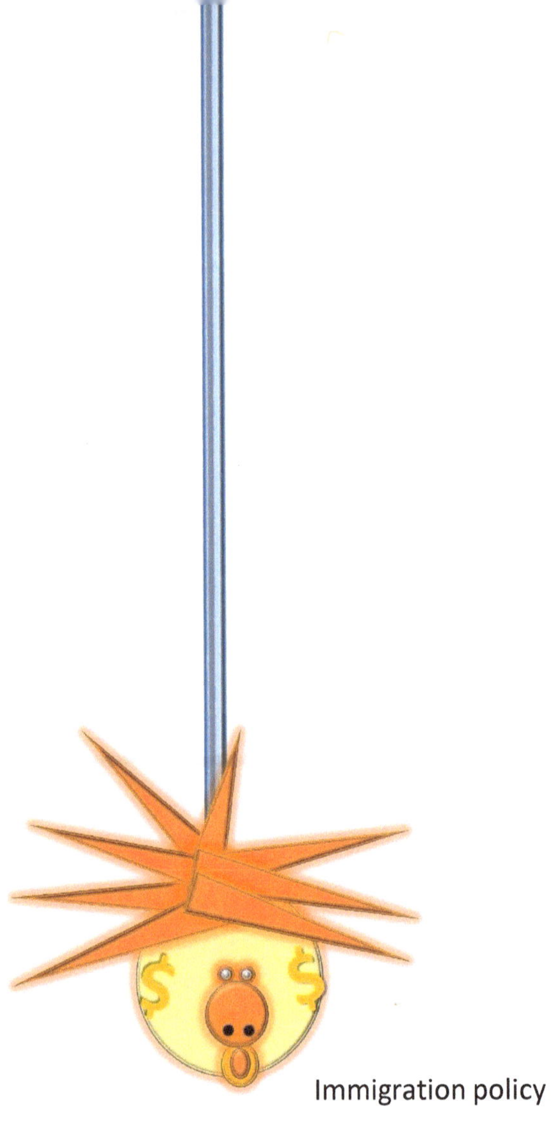

Cruelty→genocide

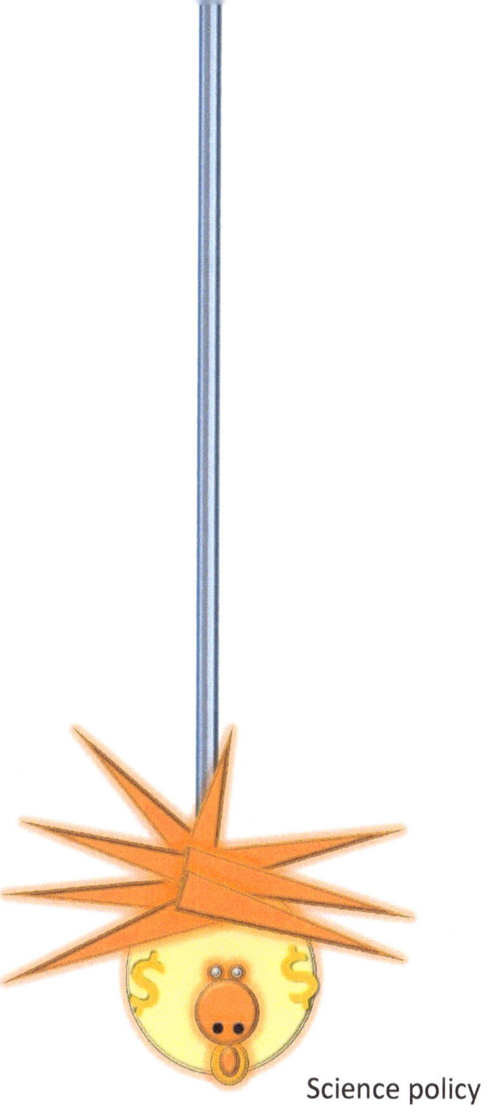

Science policy

Apologies to Walt Kelly

"It's what we don't understand that's most dangerous!"

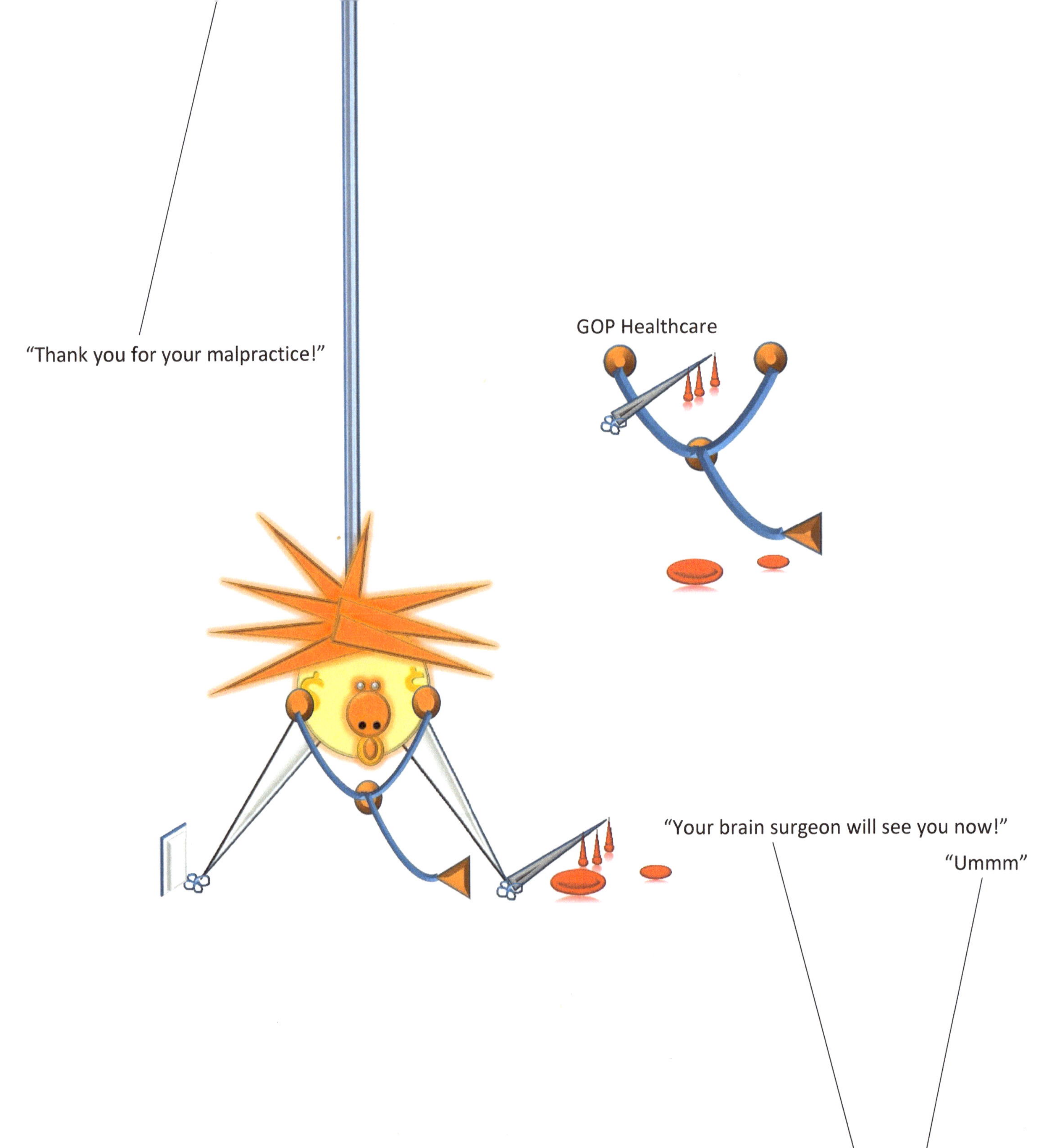
"Thank you for your malpractice!"
GOP Healthcare
"Your brain surgeon will see you now!"
"Ummm"

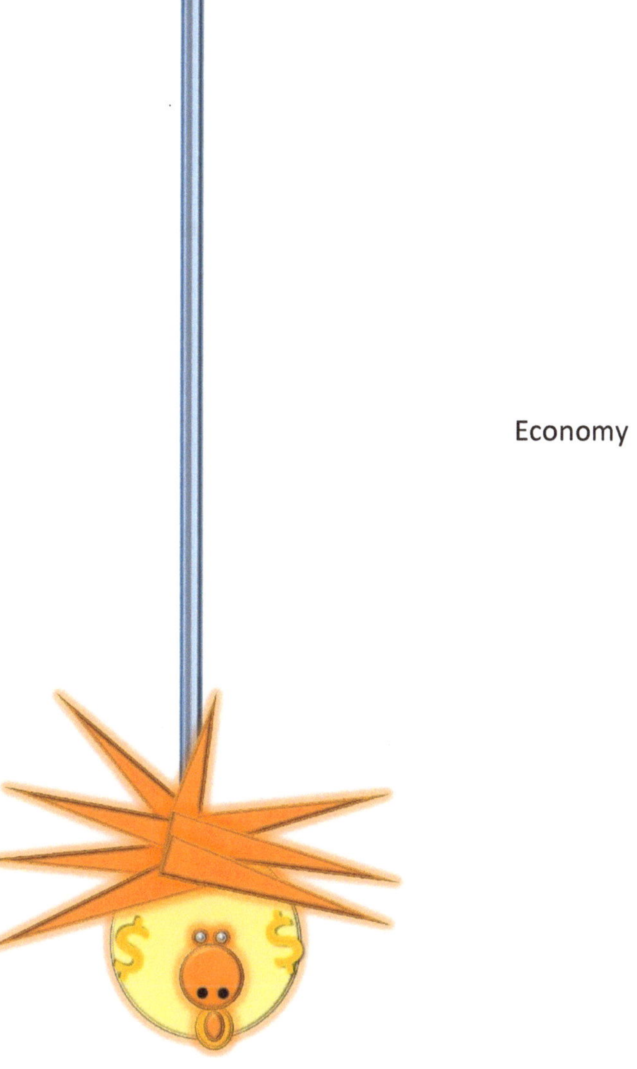

Economy

"Engorging the filthy rich with stolen wealth means prosperity!"*

*(4 me)!

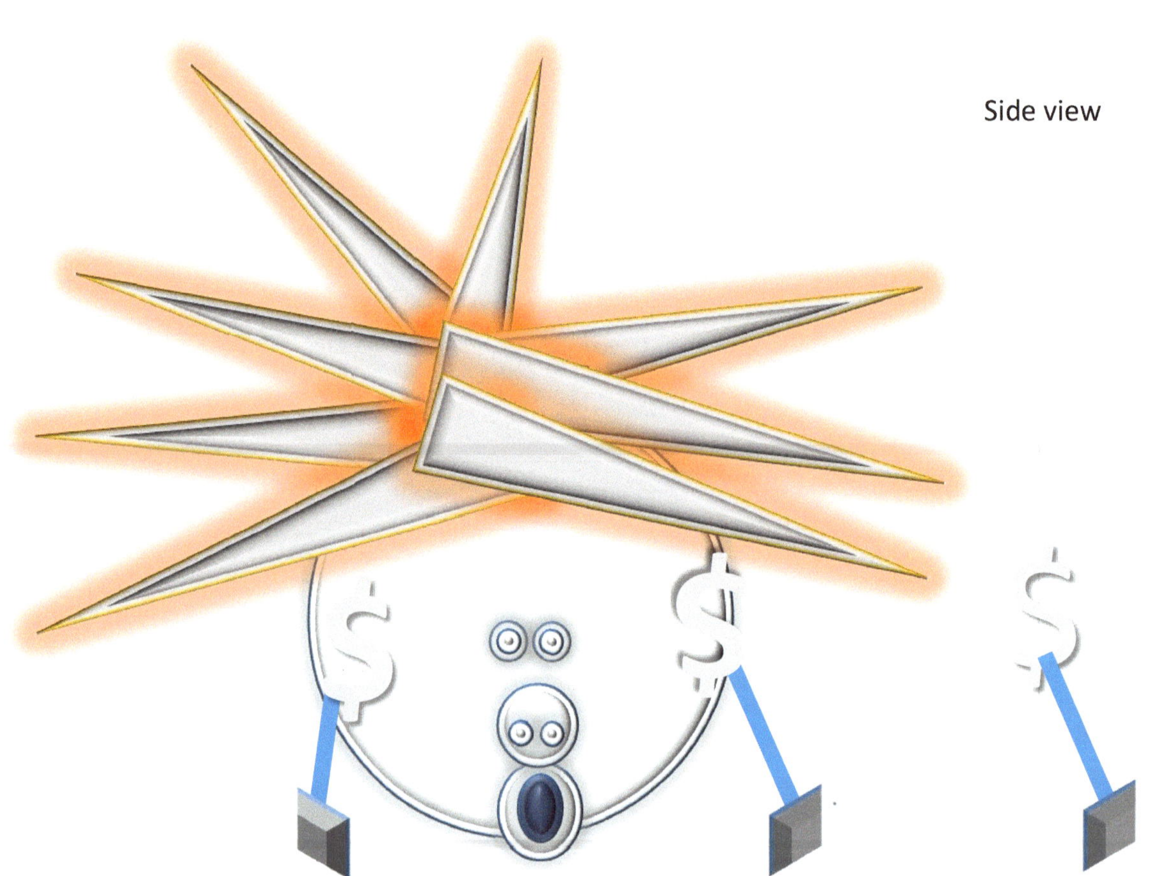
Side view

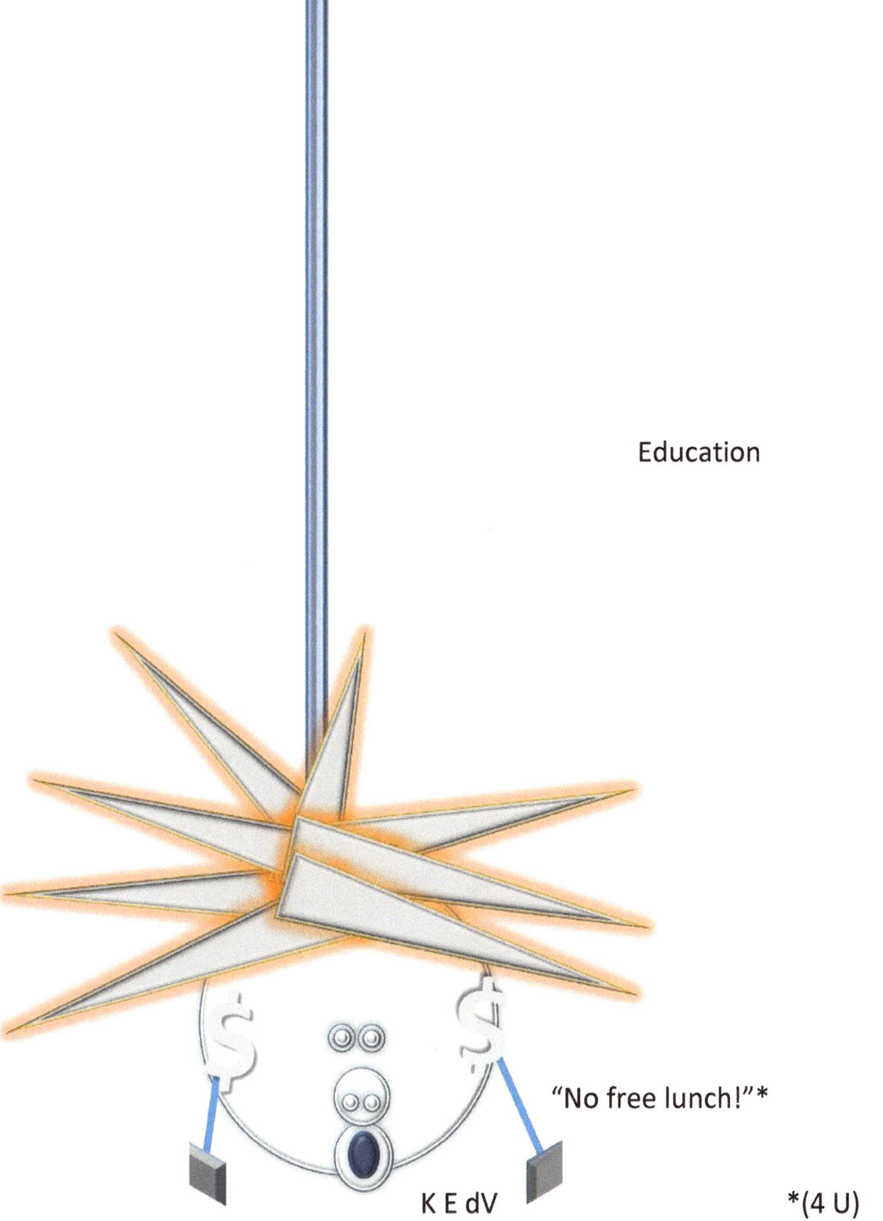

Education

*(4 U)

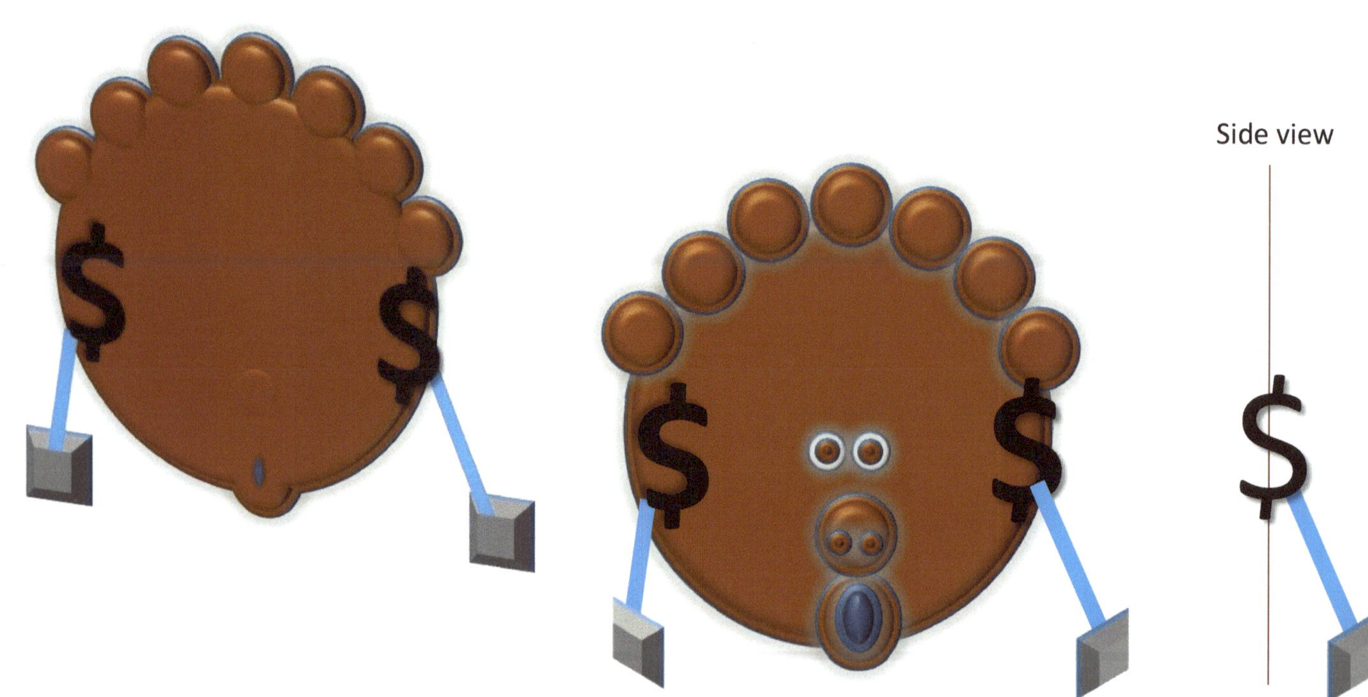

Side view

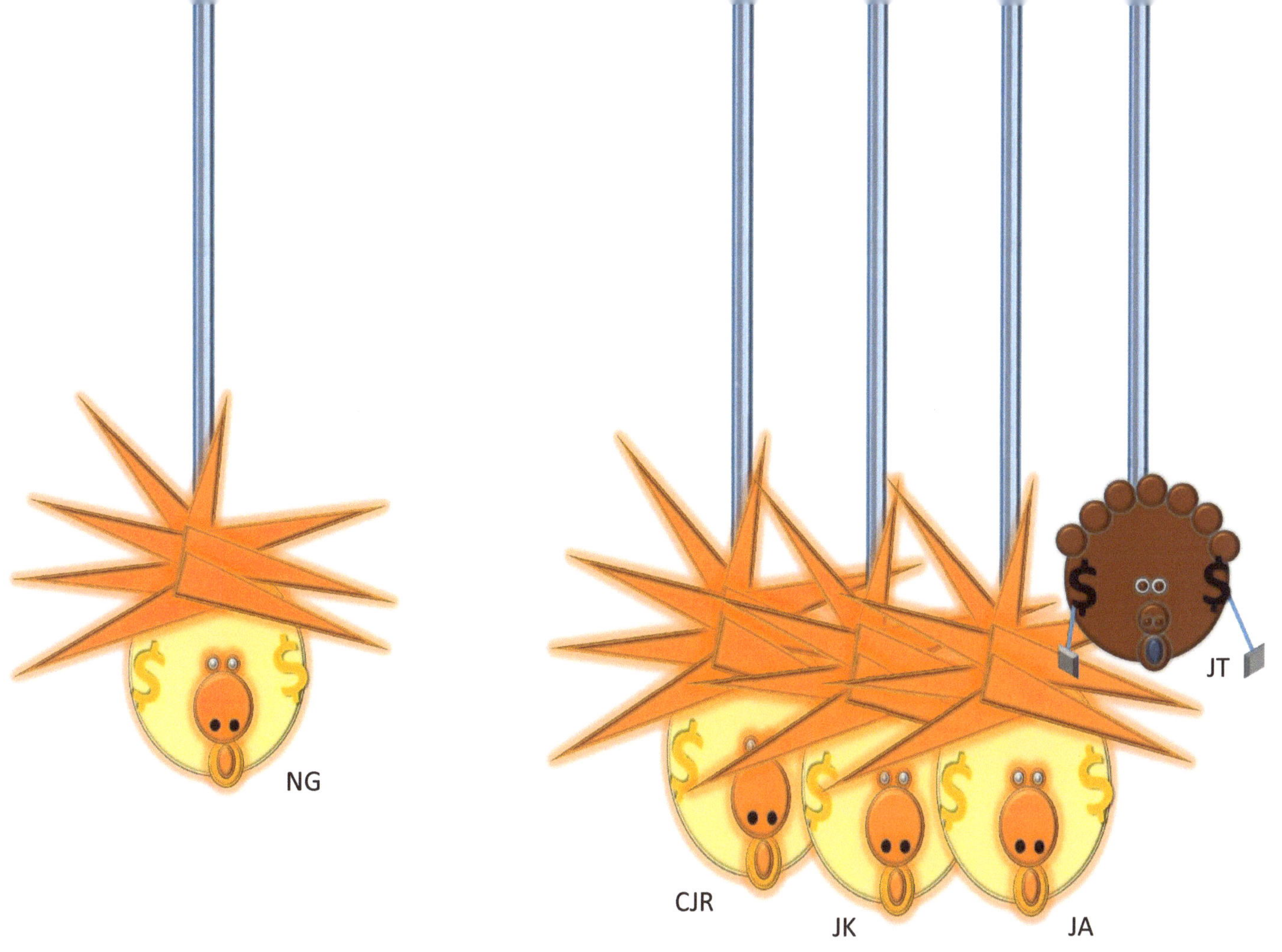
NG
+ 4 others
CJR
JK
JA
JT
SC
"The scales of justice tilt far to the fascist ultraright!"

USA (2017)

The fascist dictatorship of little minds

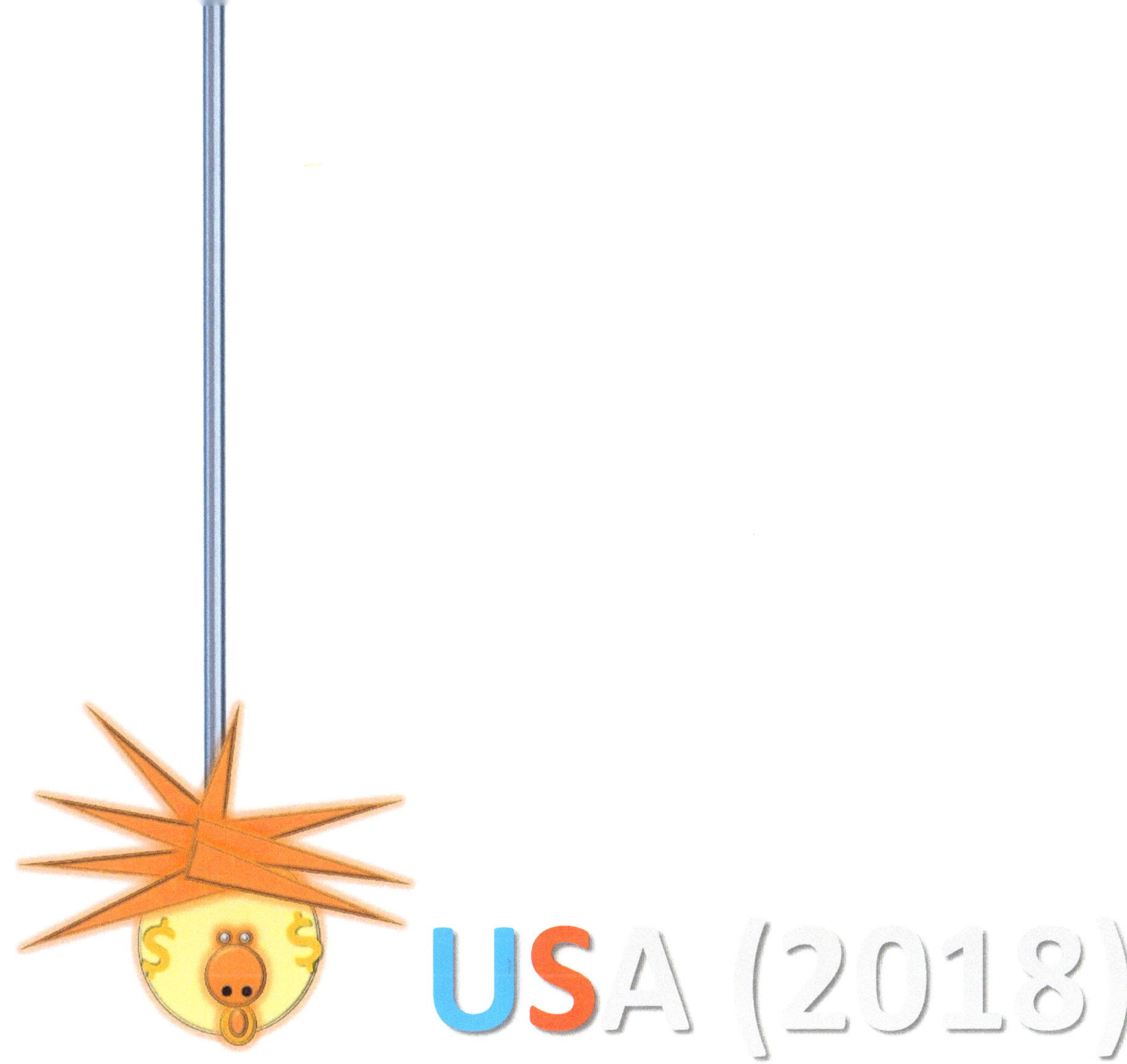

USA (2018)
The fascist dictatorship of little minds

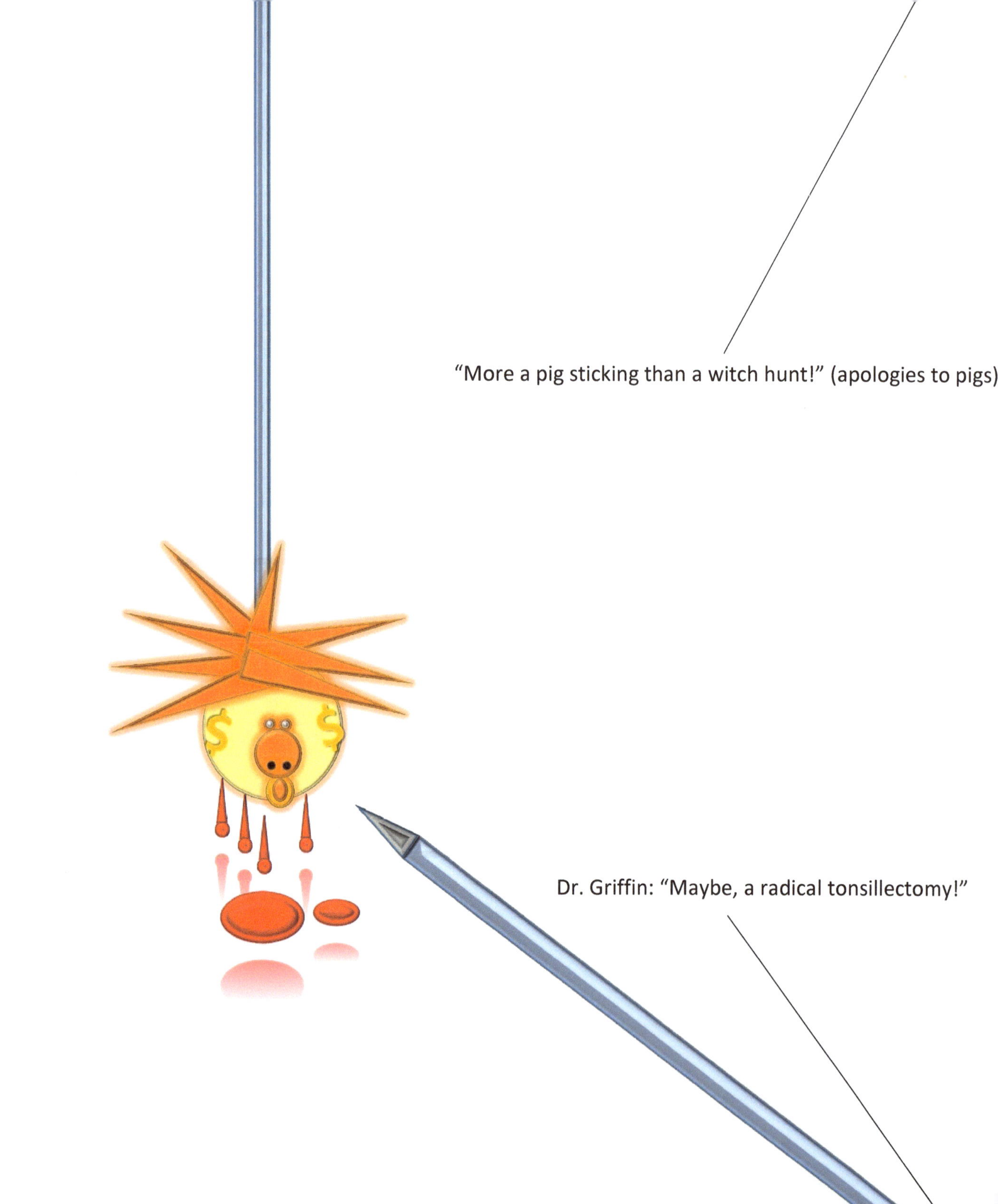

"More a pig sticking than a witch hunt!" (apologies to pigs)
Dr. Griffin: "Maybe, a radical tonsillectomy!"

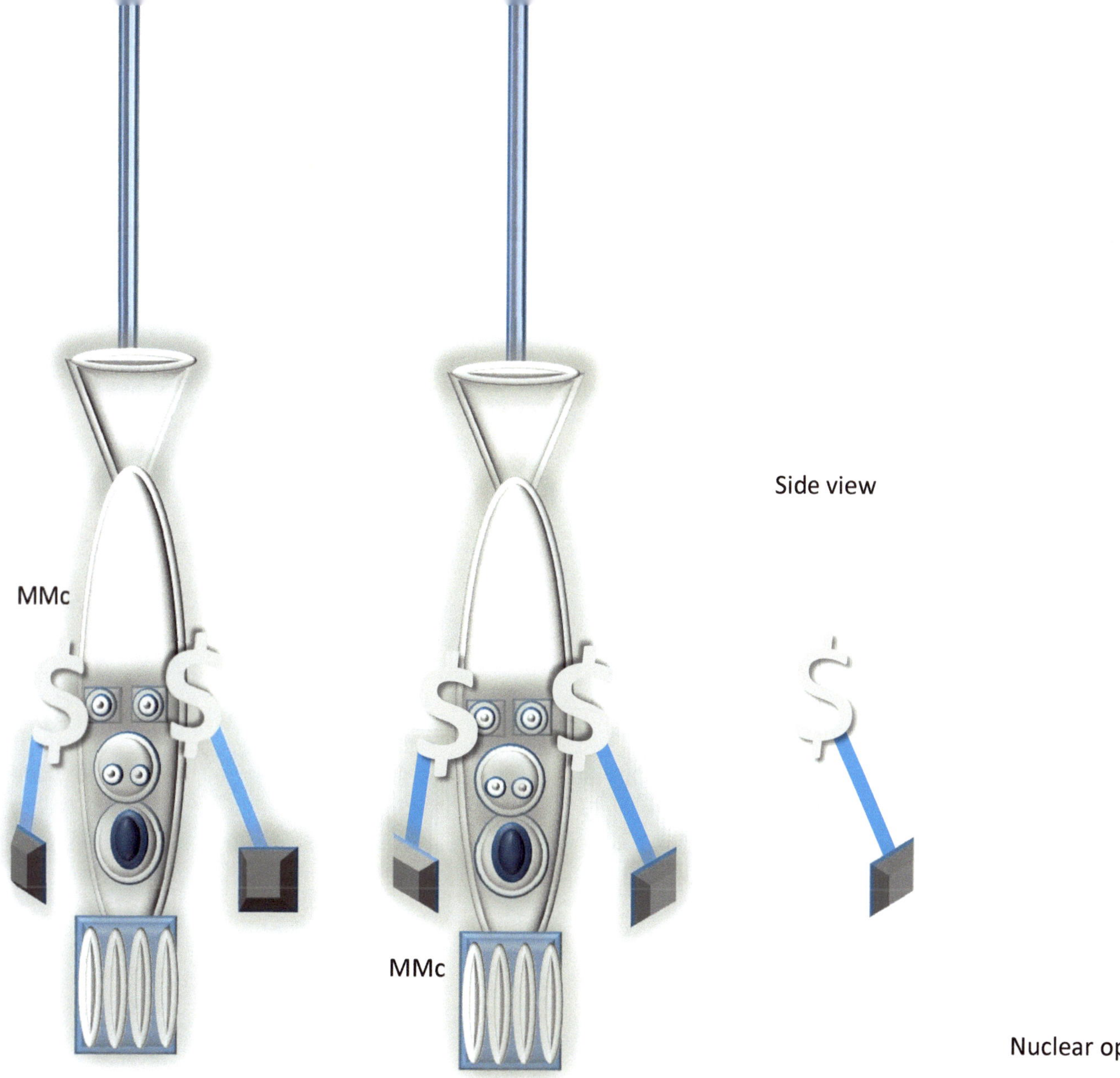

MMc
$
$
MMc
$
$
Side view
$
Nuclear option

Neoliberalism/Neoconservatism/Neofascism
Corporate DEMs
Theft motivated by greed
Financial Crime

Barack Obama

Hillary Clinton

Fascism
GOP/DJT/Alt-right/KKK/Nazis/Tea
Racism
Treason
Bigotry
Theft
Genocide
Slavery
Rape
Corporate Crime
Hate Crime
Hate Speech
Financial Crime
Bought Elections
Stolen Elections
All Right Justified

Moderates
DEMs
Bernie Sanders
One Payer
Guaranteed Income
Living Wage
Affordable College
Affordable Insurance
Honorable Retirement
Honorable Employment
Environmental protection

USA (2017)
USA (2018)

>TRUMP==TREASON

[1]   TRUE

[1]   SAD

[1]   IMPEACH

Times of Trumpel

When we find
Ourselves
In Times
Of Trumpel
Brother Comey
Comes to Thee
Speaking Words
Of Wisdom
Let it Be

(with apologies)
(not to DJT)

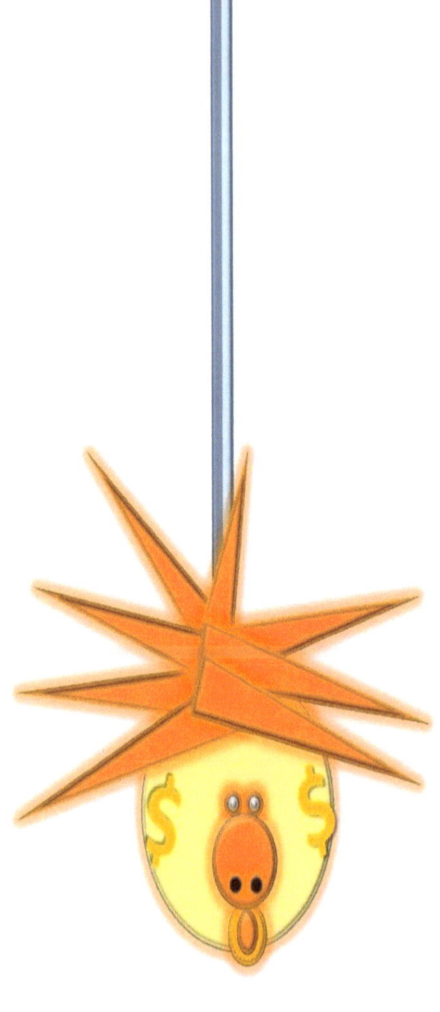

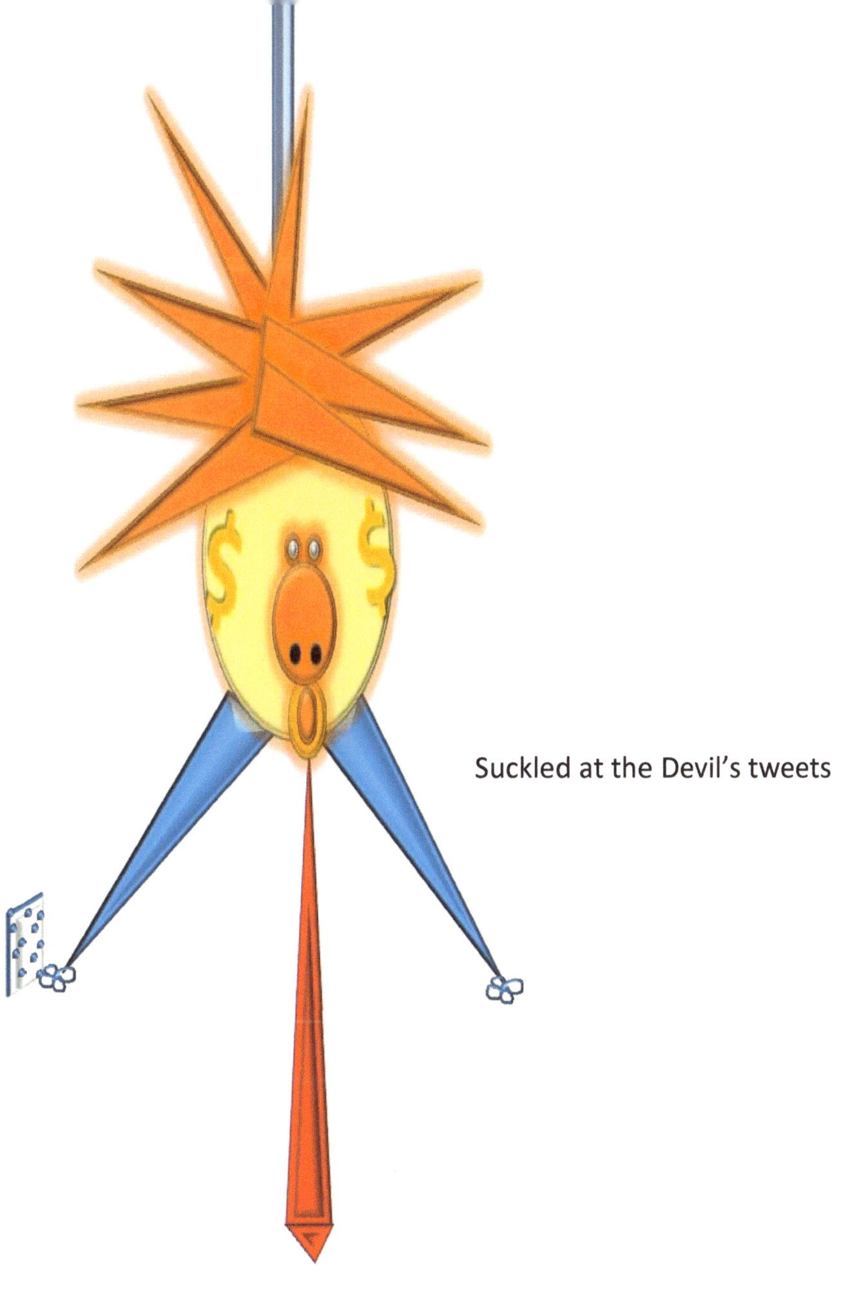

Suckled at the Devil's tweets

Sing: "10 *fascists creeping!*"

Maybe 60 years ago we coulda.

How to avoid *fascist creep*

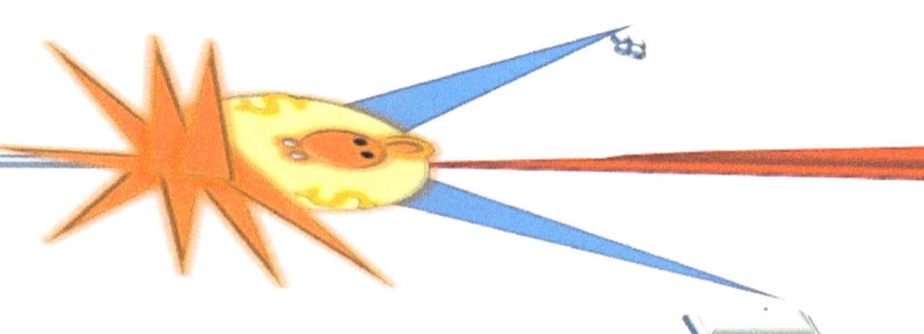

Actually, we don't know how to avoid *fascist creep*
Sad

"Wish we did!"

Sing: *"9 lords a leaping!"*

How high the wrecking ball

How to avoid *fascist creep*

More of a *fascist avalanche*

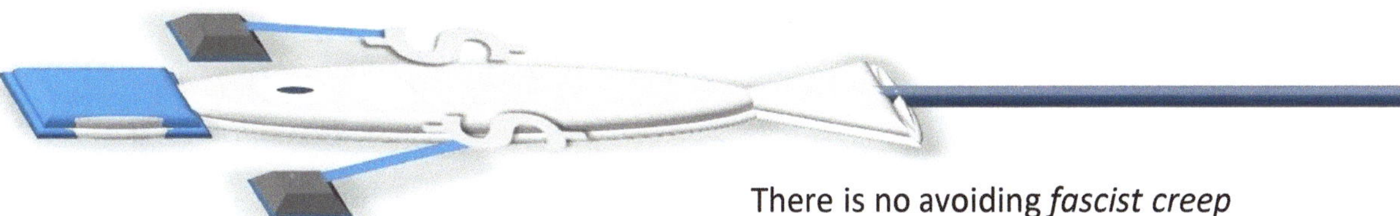

There is no avoiding *fascist creep*

Sad

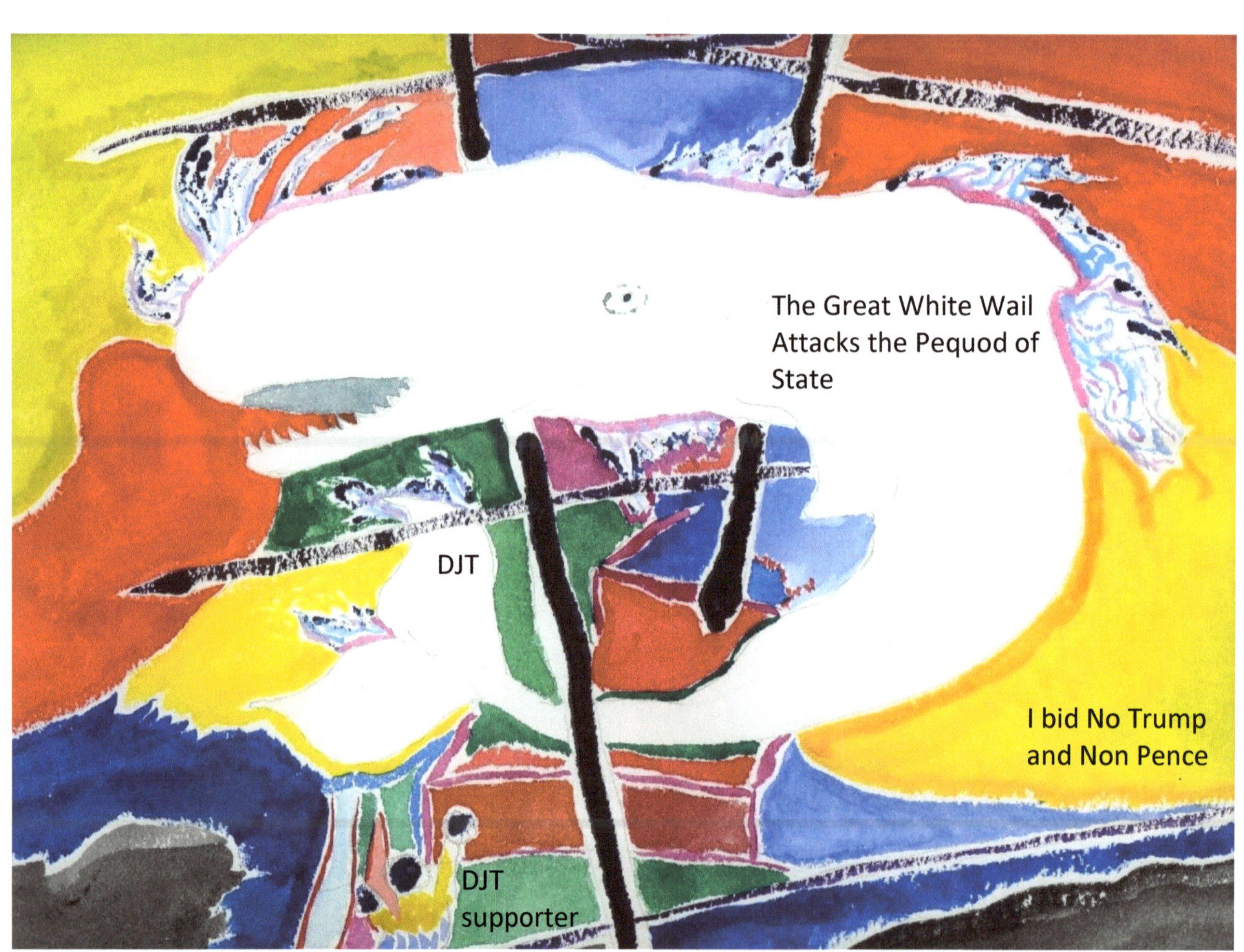

The Great White Wail
Attacks the Pequod of
State
DJT
I bid No Trump
and Non Pence
DJT
supporter